Paris Weekend with Two Kids

A Step-By-Step Travel Guide About What to See and Where to Eat
(Amazing Family-Friendly Things to Do in Paris When You Have Little Time)

By

Hassan Osman

Paris in a Weekend with Two Kids: A Step-By-Step Travel Guide About What to See and Where to Eat (Amazing Family-Friendly Things to Do in Paris When You Have Little Time)
Copyright © 2018 by Hassan Osman.

Liability Disclaimer and FTC Notice
The purpose of this book is to provide the user with general information about the subject matter presented. This book is for entertainment purposes only. This book is not intended, nor should the user consider it, to be legal advice for a specific situation. The author, company, and publisher make no representations or warranties with respect to the accuracy, fitness, completeness, or applicability of the

contents of this book. They disclaim any merchantability, fitness warranties, whether expressed or implied. The author, company, and publisher shall in no event be held liable for any loss or other damages, including but not limited to special, incidental, consequential, or other damages. This disclaimer applies to any damages by any failure of performance, error, omission, interruption, deletion, defect, delay in operation or transmission, computer malware, communication line failure, theft or destruction or unauthorized access to, or use of record, whether for breach of contract, tort, negligence, or under any other cause of action.

By reading this book, you agree that the use of it is entirely at your own risk and that you are solely responsible for your use of the contents. The advice of a competent legal counsel (or any other professional) should be sought. The author, company, and publisher do not warrant the performance, effectiveness or applicability of any sites or references listed in this book. Some links are affiliate links. This means that if you decide to make a purchase after clicking on some links, the author will make a commission. All references and links are for information purposes only and are not warranted for content, accuracy, or any other implied or explicit purpose.

Table of Contents

Introduction

Paris can be quite overwhelming with kids.

There is so much to do and see that you can go overboard on the planning.

Last summer, I spent a few days in Paris with my wife and two little girls (aged eight and four), and we had a fantastic time. We visited everything we wanted to visit in a short time period.

This book is a short guide that will help you plan your own trip. You get a step-by-step weekend itinerary with pointers about what to do and where to eat. You'll also get food recommendations and must-see highlights to make it a great trip for you and your kids.

Quick side note: If you've read my other book, Rome in a Weekend with Two Kids, you'll find a lot of the early material in this book quite similar. That's because a lot of the planning methods, phone applications, and things to buy are mostly similar in both Paris and Rome. You can skip ahead to the itinerary if you'd like to save some time.

Why Read This Book?

I'm not an expert on travel, and I'm definitely not an expert on Paris.

So why read a book written by a novice like me?

Here are three reasons why:

1) It's a short book

I like to write books that I personally enjoy reading: short and to the point. When I was researching information about visiting Paris with my kids, I didn't find what I was looking for. Most books were either too long or too detailed. All I cared about was whether something would be worth my entire family's time and whether we could fit that into our short trip. Because I didn't find a book that met my needs, I wrote this one.

2) It's thoroughly researched and planned

My day job is a project management office manager at Cisco Systems (lawyer-required note: views expressed in this guide are my own). In other words, I plan *everything*. When I was preparing for my trip, I read hundreds of online reviews and blog posts about things to do. I also read a few books about traveling in Paris with children, and I asked friends and colleagues what they personally enjoyed while on their trips. I then cross-checked all those recommendations to balance the must-see highlights with the family-friendly destinations. The end product of all that analysis is in this book.

3) It helps with avoiding FOMO and FOBO

FOMO stands for "Fear of Missing Out" and FOBO stands for "Fear of Better Options." FOMO and FOBO are your enemies during travel because they add unwanted stress. With only a few days, you will undoubtedly feel like you're going to miss out on something that wasn't part of your plan. This book will help you minimize both FOMO and FOBO because the research has been done on your behalf.

Some caveats

Here are a few things I'd like to point out before you continue reading:

- **This is NOT an extensive travel guide**. This book is not meant to cover everything you can possibly do in Paris. It is designed to solve a specific problem for parents who have limited time to plan for their trip. This means that a few activities and landmarks have been intentionally left out. For example, the Palace of Versailles is not listed anywhere in the itinerary because every review I read stated that it's not the most family-friendly destination due to long wait lines and very little entertainment value for kids. Moreover, Disneyland Paris is also not included in this book because that's an obvious kid-friendly destination that would take up an entire day from your weekend. Places like these have been left out.

- **You can do everything in two full days**. This step-by-step guide is designed for a full weekend, starting on a Friday afternoon and continuing through Sunday evening (i.e., two and a half days). However, I built the plan to be flexible enough that it can be completed in just two days if you have to (e.g., Saturday morning through Sunday evening). That's because I have intentionally included an extra half day as a backup.

- **The activities are gender-neutral**. I have two little girls, and I planned my trip with them in mind. However, the activities are gender-neutral and work for both boys and girls. The activities also work if you have more than two kids.

- **The itinerary is summer-specific**. We visited Paris in late June, so the itinerary focuses on summer activities. Although most of the same landmarks and restaurants could be visited during winter as well, keep in mind that things like public parks might be less exciting during the colder months.

With that, let's get started with your trip!

Your Free Bonus

As a thank you for purchasing this book, I have included a free gift for you.

I have put together a small PDF file that shows you several cool maps of everything I cover in this book.

The maps highlight the different zones, landmarks, and walking paths in Paris that I discuss in my step-by-step plan.

You don't *need* to download this complimentary PDF file, as all the information you need is listed in the text.

However, it is a great supplement that lets you visually see the different places I refer to, especially since it's presented in the same day-by-day format listed in this book.

Visit the following page to download your free bonus:

www.thecouchmanager.com/piwbonus

Three Things to Do Before Your Trip

Here are three things that I recommend you do before your trip:

1) Download these free phone applications (iPhone or Android)

Google Maps – This was my go-to phone application that I used most of the time in Paris. Google Maps is the best GPS navigation app that gives you addresses for all your landmarks and shows you the shortest path to walk from one place to another. It also highlights where you are if you're ever lost.

TripAdvisor – This application gives you user-generated reviews and pictures of restaurants and things to do in Paris. It uses your location to send you personalized recommendations of nearby places based on input by other travelers. I also used it whenever I wanted to read about famous historic sites that were around us.

Google Translate – This app translates text for over 100 languages, and the French to

English translation is seamless. It can even translate conversations *on the fly* while you and a foreign language speaker are talking into the app. The most impressive feature, however, is the instant camera translation. You simply point the camera at a French phrase on a street sign or menu, and it instantly translates the text for you by adding a live-text layer on top.

Make sure you download all these apps ahead of time and familiarize yourself with their features *before* you get to Paris. The last thing you want to do is waste valuable time figuring out how to use them *while* you're in Paris.

Also, note that these apps require access to the Internet to work, so sign up for an international data plan before you go, or purchase a local mobile phone data plan when you arrive.

2) Buy the following essentials

I won't get into a laundry list of things to buy for your trip, but here are a few items that were extremely helpful for us when we got there:

Travel ID bracelets – It takes a split second

for you to lose sight of your kids in touristy places. Buy a few disposable travel ID bracelets that the children can wear around their wrists or ankles in case they go missing. You can write down the name of your hotel, phone number, and any other information for law enforcement to contact you.

Hats & comfortable shoes – You'll be doing a lot of walking in Paris. Dress appropriately by wearing breathable hats and comfortable walking shoes, especially in mid-summer when the weather gets quite warm.

Rain ponchos or light jackets – Paris has very unpredictable weather. One minute, you'll have the sun up and shining, and, a few minutes later, it starts pouring and the temperature drops a few degrees. It's a good idea to carry light jackets and/or rain ponchos so that you're prepared.

Portable battery pack – If you're going to use your smartphone for navigation and for photos, you'll definitely drain your battery throughout the day. A portable battery pack will let you charge your phone (and other devices) on the go and avoid wasting time waiting for it to recharge.

International chargers/travel adapters

(110V vs 220V) – If you live in the U.S., then your electronic jacks will not fit into the European ones, so you'll need an adapter to be compatible. Also, if your device isn't dual-voltage ready (accepts 110V and 220V), then you'll also need a transformer.

Backpack & small number lock – Everyone warns of pickpockets in Paris who can snatch your wallet or phone in an instant. We carried a backpack and kept all our money and valuables tucked safely inside with a number lock on the zipper. Although unlocking and locking the backpack made it a bit of a hassle every time we needed to pay for something, it was much better than having to check our pockets every two minutes to make sure we didn't get robbed. Get a backpack that has pouches on the sides to carry your kids's water bottles.

Travel credit card & Euros – To avoid foreign transaction fees, sign up for a credit card that waives them for you. A couple that I've used are the Barclaycard Arrival Plus Card and Chase Sapphire Preferred Card. Another good idea is to purchase Euros before your trip (your local bank can provide this service). Although it's usually cheaper to purchase Euros after you land in Paris, having a couple hundred Euros in your pocket before you arrive is definitely a good idea—especially for the cab from the airport.

3) *Get your kids excited about the trip*

The final thing you should do before your trip is to get your kids excited about it early on so that they're passionately looking forward to it.

You can do that by sharing with them what you're going to do and see ahead of time.

For example, show them images of the Arc de Triomphe or Eiffel Tower using Google's image search. Or use Wikipedia to share interesting tidbits about the landmarks you'll see.

For young readers, you can even purchase an age-appropriate travel book that they can read themselves. *Kids' Travel Guide – France & Paris* was one that my eight-year-old particularly enjoyed.

Any investment in time to get them excited early on will definitely pay off later during your visit.

How I Planned the Weekend

Here's the strategy I followed to plan the weekend. You can skip this chapter if you want to, but I wanted to share my approach so that you get an idea of how to go about planning your own weekend if you'd like to make any changes.

First, I read a few books—and hundreds of reviews and blog posts—about places in Paris that were kid friendly.

I then separated the "must-see" landmarks from the "nice-to-see" ones based on personal preference and how family friendly they were. I also researched fun things to do (like tours or activities) and places to eat.

My approach to separating these two lists was simple. I wanted to do things that were authentic to France and Paris. When I came across things like the Notre-Dame Cathedral (one of the most famous churches in the world) or Laduree (the #1 ranked macaron shop in France), those went on the "must-see" list because there was no way we could experience them anywhere else.

However, when I came across things like the Menagerie du Jardin des plantes (a zoo in Paris) or Il Etait Un Square (a restaurant known for its tasty hamburgers), those went on the "nice-to-see" list because we could visit a zoo anywhere in the world, and eat awesome burgers back in the U.S. These attractions would serve as back-up destinations in case our primary plan failed or we needed to take a detour.

After that, I started plotting "must-see" landmarks and activities on a map and grouping them in zones to make our itinerary as efficient as possible. I also included places to eat along those paths.

Based on all of that, I ended up with four zones:

- **Zone 1**: Arc de Triomphe, Champs-Elysees, Jardin des Tuileries, and the Eiffel Tower
- **Zone 2**: Louvre Museum and Laduree
- **Zone 3**: Centre Pompidou, Notre-Dame Cathedral, and the Latin Quarter
- **Zone 4**: Sacre Coeur, Place du Tertre, and Montmartre

Each zone includes "must-see" landmarks and activities that are within walking distance of each other (or a quick train ride) and can be visited within half a day.

On Friday afternoon, we did Zone 1. On Saturday, we did Zone 2 in the morning and Zone 3 in the afternoon. Then, on Sunday morning, we did Zone 4.

We left Sunday afternoon as a backup for unforeseen events, like getting hit with bad weather one day or waking up late on another.

In between zones, we took a break from the walking to go back to our hotel and relax. We stayed at the Le Meridien Etoile Hotel (address: *81 Boulevard Gouvion Saint-Cyr, 75848 Cedex 17, 75017 Paris, France*), which is close to Zone 1.

For transportation, we went in and out of the zones by the underground metro because that was the most practical for us as a family. The Paris Metro system is very convenient, and we were never more than a five-minute walk away from a station when we needed one. You can purchase tickets at any station, but it can get confusing if you're new to it. A single, one-way trip costs €1.90 for adults and €0.95 for children under 10 (children under 4 travel for free). Day passes are also available, although prices can vary widely depending on a range of factors.

Read up on the transit system ahead of time on the RATP (the public transport operator of Paris) website at *https://www.ratp.fr/en* so that you understand how everything works.

In the next five chapters, I cover exactly what we did during each half-day.

Friday Afternoon

Spend your Friday afternoon in Zone 1, which includes the Arc de Triomphe, Champs-Elysees, and Eiffel Tower. You'll get a great first impression of the city and taste some amazing hot chocolate. We left the hotel at around 4:00 p.m. and returned around 10:30 p.m., so we spent around six hours in this zone.

Arc de Triomphe

What is it? Famous monument
Address: *Place Charles de Gaulle, 75008 Paris, France*
Hours: Mon–Sun, 10:00 a.m.–varies (closing time is between 10:30 p.m. & 11:00 p.m. depending on the month; see *www.arcdetriompheparis.com* for more details)
Admission: €8.00 for adults; children under 17 are free
Recommended Duration: About 1 hour

Start at one of the most iconic monuments in Paris. The Arc de Triomphe—or Triumphal Arc—was constructed to honor everyone who fought for France during previous wars. The Arc is located in the center of a roundabout of twelve intersecting avenues, and it is glorious. The first reaction kids have when seeing it for the first time is that it is much larger than they assumed from looking at the pictures.

I highly recommend you visit the inside of the Arc. There is an €8.00 entrance fee for adults (kids are free), and it's a bit of a hike to get to the top. The Arc is nearly ten stories high, and the only way to reach the terrace is through a spiral staircase, which can get very tiring for you and the kids.

However, after doing a lot of early research before our trip, nearly all parents recommend that you visit the Arc's terrace instead of the Eiffel Tower floors because the lines are shorter, the visit is faster, and the view is much nicer for children because it's at a lower level.

The reviews were right. The view from the top was breathtaking and so much fun for the kids. The coolest part was looking down at the traffic and seeing people and cars travel in and out of the 12 avenues. Make sure you point out the Champs-Elysees for your children to let them know that's where you'll be going next. The most exciting thing about the view was the Eiffel Tower in the background. You get hit with a jolt of surrealism when you see the tower for the very first time in real life, especially after seeing so many pictures of it.

As you make your way down from the Arc (through another spiral staircase), there's a nice gift shop that sells replicas of the Arc as souvenirs.

After you exit, make sure you check out the torch at the base, which is an eternal flame that burns continuously to honor unidentified soldiers who died in France's wars.

Champs-Elysees

What is it? Popular street
Address: *Avenue des Champs-Élysées, 75008 Paris, France*
Hours: Mon–Sun, 24 hours a day
Admission: Free
Recommended Duration: About 30 minutes

After the Arc de Triomphe, walk east on the Champs-Elysees, a famous avenue in Paris that is full of retail shops and restaurants. The street is around 2 km (1.2 mi) long and 70 meters (230ft) wide, and it has this grandiose, royal feel to it. It is littered with luxury brand shops such as Louis Vuitton and Hermes, as well as common international brands such as Gap, H&M, and Banana Republic.

The street can get crowded because it's a tourist magnet, but it was amusing for the kids to do some people watching and absorb the vibe of the city. They also loved looking back at the Arc de Triomphe every few minutes to see it shrink in size behind them.

Spend some time doing some window shopping along the avenue.

As you keep walking, there's a French toy store slightly off-street called La Grande Recre (address: *126 Rue la Boétie, 75008 Paris, France*) and a Disney Store close by (address: *44 Av. des Champs-Élysées, 75008 Paris, France*), which are worth a visit if you're interested.

Angelina

What is it? Famous teahouse
Address: *226 Rue de Rivoli, 75001 Paris, France*
Hours: Mon–Fri, 7:30 a.m.–7:00 p.m. | Sat–Sun, 8:30 a.m.–7:00 p.m.
Price: €8.20 for the hot chocolate/€9.30 for the Mont Blanc

Recommended Duration: About 30 minutes

As you continue on the Champs-Elysees, keep walking until you hit the Place de la Concorde and then make a left. When you get to the end of the street, make a right to continue on the Place de la Concorde, which becomes Rue de Rivoli. Angelina will be a few blocks on your left.

Walking from the Arc de Triomphe to Angelina will take a little over 30 minutes, so if you think it'll be too tiring for your kids, you can hop into the metro and get out at Tuileries Station. Angelina is a short walk from there.

Angelina is ranked as the #1 teahouse in Paris, and their tea room has a gorgeous Parisian style. They serve a light selection of salads and sandwiches, so you can have a quick light dinner there assuming the line isn't too long (wait times can run an hour or more). Try the Croque-Madame or any of their specialty croissants, which have excellent reviews.

If the dine-in line is too long, there's a second "to-go" line which moves fairly quickly, where you can pick up two things that Angelina is super famous for. The first is their heavenly old-fashioned hot chocolate, which is called l'Africain. This was the best hot chocolate any of us have ever tasted, and the kids went crazy for it. It was super rich and thick—like drinking a gourmet chocolate bar.

The second is a house special pastry called the Mont Blanc, which is a not-too-sweet dessert made out of meringue, Chantilly cream, and chestnut cream vermicelli. Honestly, the Mont Blanc was kind of underwhelming to me, and I didn't think it lived up to the hype, but it's so popular that you have to try it out!

Jardin des Tuileries

What is it? Public garden
Address: *113 Rue de Rivoli, 75001 Paris, France*
Hours: Mon–Sun, 7:00 a.m.–varies (closing time depends on the season; see *https://en.parisinfo.com/paris-museum-monument/71304/Jardin-des-Tuileries* for details)
Admission: Free
Recommended Duration: About 1.5 hours

After Angelina, cross the street to enter the Jardin des Tuileries, a beautiful public park. If you skipped having dinner at Angelina because of the long lines, there's a small cafe nearby called Happy Caffe (address: *210 Rue de Rivoli, 75001 Paris, France*) that serves delicious and inexpensive baguette sandwiches which you can eat while strolling in the park.

The Jardin des Tuileries includes plenty of things for the kids to enjoy. There are a lot of open spaces for them to run around and enjoy the birds, greenery, and statues. They can also relax on the iconic green chairs that are spread around the charming water basins.

Between June and August, the park hosts a funfair with over sixty attractions that include trampolines, slides, bumper cars, and carousels. Entrance to the funfair itself is free, but there is a charge for the rides. The most recommended attraction based on reviews is a giant Ferris wheel that towers over Paris and gives you a great view of the park and the city.

You can easily spend a few hours here, but I don't recommend staying more than an hour and a half so that you have enough time to enjoy the crown jewel of Paris: the Eiffel Tower!

Eiffel Tower

What is it? Iconic landmark
Address: *Champ de Mars, 5 Avenue Anatole France, 75007 Paris, France*
Hours: Mon–Sun, 24 hours a day
Admission: Free (there is a fee to enter the tower; see *https://www.toureiffel.paris/en* for pricing and entry times)
Recommended Duration: About 2 hours

The Eiffel Tower is a very long walk away from Jardin des Tuileries (around 40 minutes on foot), so it's best if you take the metro or a cab to get there.

An even better way is to take a cycle rickshaw—which is a bike taxi that looks like a large tricycle and is powered manually by a driver.

You'll find cycle rickshaws gathered on the east side of the Jardin de Tuileries, waiting for tourists to hire them for a quick ride.

Although they can be pricey, you can negotiate on how much you should pay, so you might get a good deal if it's not too crowded and you're persuasive. We paid around €30.00 for a ride where my wife and I sat with our daughters semi-squished in the open-air rickshaw.

The 15-minute ride was totally worth it, and the kids absolutely loved feeling the cool breeze on their faces while enjoying the picturesque views of the Seine River. As an unexpected bonus, the driver stopped along the way on the Pont Alexandre III bridge—the most extravagant bridge in Paris—to let us out and take a group family picture.

We then pedaled along to the Eiffel Tower.

It goes without saying that a trip to Paris is incomplete without a visit to the Eiffel Tower. This is one spot you don't want to miss. Just like the Arc de Triomphe, the Eiffel Tower looks much larger than you'd expect and is just as spectacular.

Spend some time walking around the base and taking pictures of the tower from different angles. Then head over to the Champs de Mars, a long green strip facing the tower where Parisians usually have a mini-picnic sipping on wine and enjoying baguettes.

As I mentioned earlier, we decided not to enter the Eiffel Tower based on the reviews we read. Apparently, the really long queues are not worth it for the kids, and the view from top is not as impressive as other views. Evidently, this is because people enjoy views that *include* the Eiffel Tower as part of the Paris skyline, like the view from the Arc de Triomphe or Sacre Coeur, and not so much *from* the Eiffel Tower itself—which kind of makes sense.

Nevertheless, if you decide to enter, make sure you purchase tickets ahead of time, because this will help manage your schedule more efficiently (see *https://www.toureiffel.paris/en* for details on tickets and hours).

After Champs de Mars, head over to Trocadero, which is an open plaza that's a short walk over the bridge. The Trocadero is scattered with street vendors and gives you a magnificent view of the tower. There are a few steps you can climb for the best vantage point.

Finally, wrap up your evening by hanging around in the Trocadero until it gets dark. At the top of every hour, the Eiffel Tower lights up for a few minutes, which is magical. We didn't want to miss this, which is why we planned our visit to the Eiffel Tower later in the afternoon, when we could enjoy views of the tower both before and after dark.

Saturday Morning

Spend your Saturday morning in Zone 2, which includes the Louvre and Laduree. We left the hotel at around 8:30 a.m. and returned around 1:30 p.m., so we spent about five hours in this zone.

Louvre Museum

What is it? Famous museum
Address: *Rue de Rivoli, 75001 Paris, France*
Hours: Wed & Fri, 9:00 a.m.–9:45 p.m. | All other days, 9:00 a.m.–6:00 p.m.
Admission: €15.00 per adult; children under 18 are free
Recommended Duration: About 3 to 4 hours

Start your Saturday morning at the Louvre, one of the most famous art and history museums in the world.

The Louvre is enormous and has over 30,000 works of art that are divided into eight different curatorial departments. To give you a sense of how big it is, if you wanted to visit every exhibit and spend only ten seconds on each piece of art, then you'd need to stay eight hours a day for over ten days to view it all!

So there's no way you can see everything, and you'll have to be strategic about what you'll see in the three to four hours you have.

The Louvre opens at 9:00 a.m., and security lines can eat up your time. To avoid a long wait, do not enter through the main pyramid entrance, which everyone gravitates to. Instead, purchase your tickets ahead of time from the website at *https://www.louvre.fr/en/*, and enter through a side entrance called Passage Richelieu where the lines are much shorter. Passage Richelieu is right across the street from the Palais Royal Musee du Louvre metro station.

There are a couple of crepe kiosks close to that entrance for a quick breakfast. If you'd rather have a sit-in breakfast, there's a café in the Louvre after you enter called Café Mollien that has a terrace overlooking the pyramid at the center of the museum (I would suggest you visit the café even if you don't want to eat, just for the view).

When you're inside the main lobby of the museum, my recommendation is to choose one section, and spend most of your time there, while targeting a few specific pieces from the other sections that you definitely want to see. We spent the majority of our time in the Egyptian Antiquities Department (in the Sully Wing) because my older daughter was studying about the Pharaohs at school, but we also visited a few other sections for select pieces.

Here are a few art pieces that are quite popular across the museum:

- **Mona Lisa** (Denon Wing, First Floor, Room 6) – this painting by Leonardo da Vinci is the most popular piece in the entire museum (if not the world). And you can tell because of the crowds surrounding it. Do not miss it!
- **Venus de Milo** (Sully Wing, Ground Floor, Room 7) – this Greek sculpture is believed to be of Aphrodite, the goddess of beauty and love. It's famous for its missing arms.
- **The Winged Victory of Samothrace** (Denon Wing, Ground Floor, Staircase) – this large Hellenistic sculpture represents Nike, the winged goddess of victory, standing on a ship.
- **The Wedding Feast at Cana** (Denon Wing, First Floor, Room 6) – this humongous painting, which is facing the Mona Lisa, shows a banquet

where Jesus Christ is converting water into wine.

- **The Marly Horses** (Richelieu Wing, Ground Floor, Courtyard) – these are two large and beautiful sculptures of horses being tamed.

Don't stress out about visiting every single piece (again, remember that FOMO is your enemy), because there's a high chance that your kids will start complaining and you'll want to cut your visit earlier than expected.

To minimize the possibility of this happening, read about your must-see pieces to your kids ahead of time so that you keep them excited.

Pizza Oskian

What is it? Italian restaurant
Address: *139 rue Saint Honore, 75001 Paris, France*
Hours: Mon–Fri, 11:30 a.m.–3:00 p.m., 6:00 p.m.–11:00 p.m. | Sat–Sun, 11:30 a.m.–11:30 p.m.
Price: Around €25.00 for a medium pizza and a starter
Recommended Duration: About 1 hour

After visiting the Louvre, have lunch at Pizza Oskian, a nearby restaurant that serves delicious thin crust pizzas. To get there, you'll have to exit the Louvre anywhere on its north end and walk east on Rue de Rivoli. Then make a left on Rue du Louvre, and another left on Rue Saint Honore. Pizza Oskian is a few meters on your left.

The restaurant serves authentic-style Italian pizzas and has super-friendly staff. There were several young families sitting around, so it struck us as a kid-friendly place. It also has a nice cozy feel to it. Although we wanted to try out a French restaurant, our kids were quite picky and hungry, so we opted for Italian instead.

Try the quattro formaggi (four cheese) pizza or the basil and smoked salmon pizza, which both have high reviews. Then have one of their delicious cappuccinos to finish off your meal.

Laduree

What is it? French macaron specialty shop
Address: *14 Rue de Castiglione, 75001 Paris, France*
Hours: Mon–Fri, 10:00 a.m.–7:30 p.m. | Sat–Sun, 10:00 a.m.–7:00 p.m.
Price: €2.00 for one macaron
Recommended Duration: About 20

minutes

After lunch, head over to Laduree, a dessert bakery that's a 15-minute walk away from the restaurant. To get there, head west on Rue Saint Honore and then make a slight right on Avenue de L'Opera. Make a left to continue on Rue Saint Honore. Keep walking until you reach Rue de Castiglione and then make a left. You'll see Laduree on the left.

Laduree is a famous French luxury bakery and tea house that has multiple locations around Paris. The kids will love this store because it looks like a high-end candy shop that screams with different colors. The décor and staff play the part well.

This particular shop sells their main specialty: the French macaron. These will be the most delicious macarons you have ever tasted. They are expensive, but definitely worth it.

We sampled around a dozen macarons, and every one tasted better than the one before. A few of our favorites were the Pistachio, Caramel, Raspberry, Chocolate, and Orange Blossom.

After Laduree, head over to your hotel to rest for a little bit. We found it refreshing to return to the hotel room so that the kids could rest their tired feet or take a short nap. My wife and I used that time to also relax and connect with friends and family back home.

Saturday Afternoon

After your break, spend your Saturday afternoon and evening in Zone 3, which includes the area around Centre Pompidou and Notre-Dame Cathedral. We left the hotel at around 4:00 p.m. and returned later in the evening at around 9:30 p.m., so we spent approximately five and a half hours in Zone 3.

Fontaine Stravinsky

What is it? Public fountain
Address: *2 Rue Brisemiche, 75004 Paris, France*
Hours: Mon–Sun, 24 hours a day
Admission: Free
Recommended Duration: About 20 minutes

Fontaine Stravinsky is a public fountain that sits on a shallow water basin and includes 16 sculptural pieces created by sculptors Niki de Saint Phalle and Jean Tinguely. The sculptures are all quite colorful and include representations of things such as a spiral, an elephant, a mermaid, and a clown's hat. This was a fountain that the kids were excited to see because nearly every children's book they read about Paris included a reference to these sculptures.

Honestly, the fountain itself and the nearby area is not very well preserved, but this was a nice spot to people watch and enjoy a couple of street shows in the area in front of the fountain.

Centre Pompidou

What is it? Multi-cultural complex
Address: *Place Georges-Pompidou, 75004 Paris, France*
Hours: Wed–Mon, 11:00 a.m.–9:00 p.m. (closed on Tuesdays)
Admission: €14.00 per adult; children under 18 are free
Recommended Duration: About 2 hours

Right next to Fontaine Stravinsky is Centre Pompidou, which is a contemporary art and architecture building. The kids will enjoy watching the structure because it looks like an 'inside-out' building with colorful pipes and tubes exposed on its façade.

The building hosts a public library, a museum of modern art, and a center for music, so there is a lot to see.

For kids, there are a couple of sections that offer fun activities for families. The first is the Kids Gallery, which is an exhibition area that offers interactive and educational workshops. The second is the Kids Studio, which focuses on helping little children appreciate art and become more curious. Check out the different program offerings and purchase tickets ahead of time at *https://www.centrepompidou.fr/en/* to be prepared and avoid waiting too long in line. Kids under 18 are free with paying adults.

When you enter the complex, make sure you take advantage of the transparent escalator ride, which has some amazing external views.

Amorino

What is it? Gelateria
Address: *119–121 Rue Saint-Martin, 75004 Paris, France*
Hours: Mon–Sun, 11:00 a.m.–10:00 p.m.
Price: €3.60/€5.70 for small/large (cone or cup)
Recommended Duration: About 20 minutes

After Centre Pompidou, head over to Amorino, which is across the open square right in front of the complex.

Amorino is a famous *gelateria* (ice-cream shop) known for its beautiful cone presentations. They serve gelato in flower shapes which look like artistic masterpieces *and* taste phenomenal.

Choose different flavors for your petals, so you get a sampling of several varieties. Try the raspberry, mango, and lemon flavors if you're going for a fruit-based cone, or the tiramisu, *stracciatella*, and pistachio if you're going with a cream-based one. You can also up-size to get a mini-macaron at the center of your flower.

Notre-Dame Cathedral

What is it? Historic landmark/church
Address: *6 Parvis Notre-Dame – Pl. Jean-Paul II, 75004 Paris, France*
Hours: Mon–Fri, 7:45 a.m.–6:45 p.m. | Sat–Sun, 7:45 a.m.–7:15 p.m.
Admission: Free (there is a €10.00 fee if you want to visit the towers)
Recommended Duration: About 1 hour

The Notre-Dame is listed as one of the most iconic churches in the world, and it is a must-see in Paris. It's around a 15-minute walk from Centre Pompidou. To get there, head south on Rue du Renard until you reach the Seine river, then cross over on the Pont d'Arcole Bridge. Continue on Rue d'Arcole until you reach Notre-Dame on your left.

This magnificent cathedral was built in 1345 and epitomizes French Gothic architecture. Even if you're not a huge fan of structural art, this building is so awe-inspiring that even little kids can appreciate the details on the façade (and if your kids are fans of the Disney cartoon classic "The Hunchback of Notre Dame," then they'll be extra excited about it).

Spend some time walking around the cathedral to absorb its beauty. Entrance to the Notre-Dame itself is free because it is a public church, but you'll have to wait in line to get in. Once inside, you get to enjoy the colorful stained-glass windows, which look black from the outside. You can also light a candle for a €2.00 donation. If you'd like to head up to the towers, there's a separate €10.00 ticket fee which you can purchase outside the cathedral (more details here: *http://www.notredamedeparis.fr/en/*).

Around the Notre-Dame are several street shows which were a ton of fun. On the south side, close to the Siene River, there's also a little play area for the kids to hang out.

Latin Quarter

What is it? Historic walking area
Address: *13 Rue Saint-Séverin, 75005 Paris, France*
Hours: Mon–Sun, 24 hours a day
Admission: Free
Recommended Duration: About 2 hours (including dinner time)

After Notre-Dame, head over to the Latin Quarter, which is a quaint neighborhood on the left bank of the Seine River. To get there, cross the Pont au Double Bridge and make a right on Quai de Montebello. Then make a left on Rue Saint-Julien le Pauvre, and a right on Rue de la Bucherie.

You'll get to a famous bookstore called Shakespeare & Company on your left, which is worth a quick visit (address: *37 Rue de la Bûcherie, 75005 Paris, France*). This is an old historical bookshop that is famous among book lovers. The store sells new and second-hand books, and it is known for hosting aspiring writers to sleep over in exchange for their helping out with tasks.

After Shakespeare & Company, continue on

Rue de la Bucherie, and cross the street to get to Rue de la Huchette. This is a narrow street that gives you a great taste of the Latin Quarter, which is full of souvenir shops and international restaurants. Although the Latin Quarter can get quite crowded, just walking around this place gives you a genuine vibe that you'll enjoy with your family.

When you're hungry, continue to walk on Rue de la Huchette and make a left on Rue Xavier Privas. Then make a right on Rue Saint-Severin and stay on the path until you reach a restaurant called La Luge on your left (address: *19 Rue Saint-Séverin, 75005 Paris, France*). This is a place that serves Raclette, a popular cheese dish in France that is typically served with baked potatoes and ham. A cheese wedge is set on a plate underneath a heat lamp which you can adjust. The cheese melts, and you can then scrape it off onto slices of fresh baguette. We had a lot of fun with the kids with this one. They also serve traditional fondue, which received some pretty good reviews.

After dinner, head back on Rue Saint-Severin and make a left on Rue de la Harpe. You'll get to a *creperie* (crepe shop) called Chez Suzette (address is: *12 Rue de la Harpe, 75005 Paris 05, France*) that serves crepes to-go from their window stall. Try any of their Nutella with banana or strawberry crepes for dessert.

Continue to stroll around the Latin Quarter as you enjoy the different scenes. If you're still feeling adventurous after all this time, there's another famous street in the Latin Quarter you can visit. It's called Rue Mouffetard and is a 15-minute walk away. This was highly recommended by reviewers for its quaint market stalls that sell French delicacies, but our kids were just too tired by this time, so we called it a night and headed back to the hotel.

Sunday Morning

Spend your Sunday morning in Zone 4, which includes Sacre-Coeur and the beautiful area of Montmartre. On this day, we left the hotel at around 8:30 a.m. and returned at around 2:30 p.m., so we spent five hours in that zone.

Le Grenier a Pain

What is it? French boulangerie (with optional behind-the-scenes tour)
Address: *38 Rue des Abbesses, 75018 Paris, France*
Hours: Thu–Mon, 7:30 a.m.–8:00 p.m. (closed Tuesdays and Wednesdays)
Price: Around €1.50 for a baguette; €100.00+ for a behind-the-scenes tour for four (pastries included)
Recommended Duration: About 1 hour

Start your Sunday morning at Le Grenier a Pain, a *boulangerie* (bakery) that offers a wide selection of pastries and breads for a delectable breakfast.

This bakery offers an optional tour where you'll get a behind-the-scenes view of an authentic Parisian boulangerie. Paris is famous for its pastries and baked treats, and we wanted to learn more about what goes into making them. At around €25.00 per person, the one-hour tour was not especially cheap, but it was totally worth it.

You'll get to see how traditional baguettes are made by French bakers. If you're lucky, and the bakery isn't too crowded, they'll let young ones help out by rolling some dough (which is what happened with our kids).

You'll also get to see how different pastries and cakes are made, including croissants and eclairs. It was fascinating to see how all the machinery worked as the guide walked us through the process. The best part is that you'll get a sample of everything at the end of your tour as a scrumptious treat.

If you're interested in the tour, you'll have to sign up in advance because the slots fill up really fast. The restaurant takes reservations through a third-party site called Viator.

Here's the link to the tour we signed up for:

http://www.thecouchmanager.com/bakery

(Note: Viator works with several boulangeries in Paris, so it's not guaranteed that you'll end up with Le Grenier a Pain because that depends on their availability. However, the reviews for all other boulangeries under this tour are positive and highlight a similar experience.)

If you decide not to sign up for the tour, Le Grenier a Pain is still an excellent spot to have a regular à la carte breakfast. Make sure you try their traditional baguettes, which won the 'Best Baguette in Paris' competition—twice!

Sacre Coeur

What is it? Popular landmark
Address: *35 Rue du Chevalier de la Barre, 75018 Paris, France*
Hours: Mon–Sun, 6:00 a.m.–10:30 p.m.
Admission: Free
Recommended Duration: About 1 hour

After Le Grenier a Pain, head over to Sacre Coeur, a famous Catholic church and minor basilica (known as the Basilica of the Sacred Heart of Paris) located at the highest point in all of Paris.

Sacre Coeur is only a seven-minute walk away from Le Grenier a Pain. However, if you add five more minutes to your trip by taking a different route (i.e., a total of 12 minutes), you'll get to enjoy a couple of stops that the kids will enjoy. You'll also get to experience the first sight of Sacre Coeur peeking from behind the narrow streets for an extra wow factor.

From Le Grenier a Pain, head east on Rue des Abbesses and make a right on Rue des Martyrs. Then make a left on Rue d'Orsel and a right on Rue Dancourt. When you get to Boulevard de Rochechouart, make a left until you get to Rue de Steinkerque, and make a left.

(Note: if you didn't have breakfast at Le Greneir a Pain, then take the metro to Anvers Station. Rue de Steinkerque is right next to it.)

Rue de Steinkerque is a narrow uphill street that is sprinkled with several shops. A few meters on the right is a store called La Cure Gourmande, which is a high-end sweet shop that sells gourmet cookies and biscuits. This shop is definitely worth a visit to check out and sample its treats. Further along the street are several souvenir shops where you can buy really cool fridge magnets and snow globes.

As you get to the end of the street, you'll see Sacre Coeur peeking at you from the top of the hill. The sight is so magnificent that tourists around you seeing it for the first time gasp simultaneously at its overwhelming beauty.

At the foot of Sacre Coeur—and right across the street from the end of Rue de Steinkerque—is an old double-decker carousel. Make sure you take a ride on it with your kids as it has a cozy 18th century feel to it.

To get to the top of Sacre Coeur, you can either take the stairs (there are about 300 of them!) or the funicular, which is a cool-looking cable car with panoramic windows. We opted for the funicular because there was no way our kids could make it up the stairs, and it was extra entertainment for the kids.

The funicular entrance is a few meters away from the carousel. As you exit the carousel, make a right on Place Saint-Pierre and you'll see it on your right. The whole ride is short (90 seconds long), and is operated by the RATP, so you can use the same tickets you use for the metro. The price is €1.90 for adults and €0.95 for children under 10 (children under 4 are free).

When you get to the top, walk over to the basilica on your right and enjoy the stunning views of Paris. This is the highest point in the city, and it makes a great spot to take pictures.

You can also enter the basilica itself (entrance is free), but we opted out of that because of the long lines.

Place du Tertre

What is it? Small square for artists
Address: *Place du Tertre, 75018 Paris, France*
Hours: Mon–Sun, 24 hours a day (artists show up early in the morning and stay late into the evening)
Price: Free
Recommended Duration: Around 1 hour

After Sacre Coer, head toward Place du Tertre, a small cobbled-stone square full of artists and cafes. It's a short, 3-minute walk away from Sacre Coer. Head west on Rue Azais, then make a right on Rue du Mont-Cenis. When you turn the corner, keep going straight for a few steps on Rue Norvins. The square will be on your left.

Place du Tertre is one of my favorite spots in Paris. If you're an art-lover, this place is like heaven. The square is packed with artists hanging out as they work on their art and display some of their pieces for sale.

There are painters, sketch artists, portraitists, and caricaturists—you name it.

The atmosphere just oozes art, and the area is referred to as the beating heart of Montmartre. You'll also find silhouette artists, who will draw your side profile using nothing but a pair of scissors and some black cardboard paper. We bought a couple of these silhouette cut-outs for our daughters, which we framed when we got back home (make sure you negotiate a price before you agree to purchase any artist work—they can easily guilt you into overpaying). After our negotiations, we paid around €15.00 for two silhouettes.

Grab a cup of coffee from one of the cafes, and spend some time walking around the square and watching artists work on their craft.

Le Petit Train de Montmartre

What is it? Little train ride in Montmartre
Address: *Place du Tertre, 75018 Paris, France*
Hours: Mon–Sun, 10:00 a.m.–7:00 p.m. during summer (other seasons vary; check *http://www.promotrain.fr/* for more details)
Price: €6.50 for adults; €4.50 for children under 12

Recommended Duration: Around 40 minutes

Right next to Place du Tertre, along Rue du Mont-Cenis where you walked in from Sacre Coeur, is a little white train parked in the corner. This is an open-air trolley that takes you for a ride around Montmartre, a gorgeous historic district. Both Sacre Coeur and Place du Tertre are in Montmartre, so you will have already tasted some of what it has to offer.

Riding the train is the best (and fastest) way to continue exploring the area. It'll also give your kids a nice break from all the walking. The train leaves every 30 minutes, and you can pay the driver directly for your tickets. The whole ride takes around 40 minutes, and it includes French background music as well as running commentary in French and English.

The guide points out several famous landmarks along the way, including Van Gogh's apartment. Montmartre sits on a large hill, so prepare for a bumpy ride as the train makes its way through the narrow curves.

The ride stops at the Moulin Rouge, which is a world-famous cabaret in Paris. Known as the night club where the can-can dance was born, it is marked by a large red windmill. On the traffic island facing the Moulin Rouge is a large circular air vent which blows pressurized air through the grate. The kids will have a blast jumping around on it as the air lifts up their clothes.

Rouge Bis

What is it? French bistro
Address: *2 Rue de Bruxelles, 75009 Paris, France*
Hours: Mon–Fri, 7:30 a.m.–2:00 a.m. | Sat–Sun, 8:00 a.m.–2:00 a.m.
Price: Around €4.00 for a pizza slice
Recommended Duration: About 1 hour

When you're ready for lunch, cross the street to get to Rouge Bis, a great French restaurant that serves authentic food.

Start with snail croquettes (if you're daring!) and duck spring rolls for an appetizer. Then go for a chicken saltimbocca or steak tartare entrée, which have stellar reviews. Finally, wrap it up with either their peach soup or brioche French toast for dessert.

After Rouge Bis, head back to the hotel to get some rest and freshen up.

Sunday Afternoon

Sunday afternoon was left as a backup to plan for events that were beyond our control. If our flight was delayed on Friday, or if it rained on Saturday, we would have used our Sunday afternoon to make up for any lost time.

We also wanted to allow for some flexibility in case we wanted to sleep in late one day or spend more time in a location because we were enjoying our time.

I highly recommend you do this as well, because it'll help you enjoy your vacation and not stress out about anything you might miss. Having a backup scheduled by design becomes especially valuable if one of your kids gets sick or cranky, and you need to deviate from your plan to get them back on track.

Assuming everything goes smoothly for you, though, you'll have an entire half-day at your disposal.

You can spend it on any of the "nice-to-see" places from your earlier list or on a return trip to a zone you already visited. Some landmarks, such as the Arc de Triomphe, have a totally different look and feel in the evening when the lights are on.

So what can you do?

Here are my recommendations.

First, go to the Seine River to take a boat tour. This was already on our "nice-to-see" list, but we didn't have the time to squeeze it in earlier on.

The best spot to start your cruise is right next to the Eiffel Tower, which is great because, as an added bonus, you get to see the tower again.

To purchase tickets, walk to the Pont d'Iena Bridge, where you'll see a set of stairs close to the river bank. As you walk down the stairs, you'll see a cashier for a cruise company called Vedettes de Paris, where you can purchase tickets (alternatively, you can also book your tickets and check out departure times ahead of time at *https://www.vedettesdeparis.fr/en/*).

There's a round-trip cruise option (around 1 hour; €16.00 per adult and €8.00 per child) and a one-way cruise option (around 30 minutes; €12.00 per adult and €5.00 per child), and both options pass by the same major highlights of the city. My recommendation is to take the one-way option because the boat will drop you off at the Pont Marie Bridge right next to the Notre-Dame Cathedral.

The boarding point for the cruise is right next to the cashier kiosk. Once onboard, make your way to the top-deck for the best views of Paris.

After the cruise, grab some of the best ice cream in Paris from Berthillon Glacier (address: *29-31 Rue Saint-Louis en l'Île, 75004 Paris, France*). This is a very famous ice cream shop that was listed on every top-ten list I researched. Try their salted caramel flavor, which seems to be their most popular flavor.

Then head toward the Luxembourg Gardens, which is a perfectly manicured public park that is around a 20-minute walk away from Berthillon Glacier (address: *29-31 Rue Saint-Louis en l'Île, 75004 Paris, France*). There are plenty of activities for the kids to do in the park, including renting model sail boats to play with in the central water basin. They also have pony rides, as well as a large playground for children to run around. Make sure you check out the Marie De Medici Fountain, which is a historic fountain with stunning sculptures located in the northeast section of the park. In the west part of the park is a mini replica of the Statue of Liberty, which is also exciting to see.

For dinner, grab some delicious sandwiches from the nearby La Parisienne Madame Bakery (address: *48 Rue Madame, 75006 Paris, France*). Try their cheese with sundried tomatoes baguette. They also serve excellent *pain aux raisins* (raisin bread) and thin apple tarts.

Then head back to the park to munch on your treats while relaxing on the benches. The Luxembourg Gardens is the best place to wrap up your vacation as you absorb the last sights of Parisians strolling around the park.

Conclusion

We just covered a step-by-step itinerary that will help you plan for your trip with your kids.

One suggestion I have is to go back to the beginning of the book and re-read the "Three Things to Do Before Your Trip" section. This will help you plan ahead and make sure you'll get the most out of your trip.

Then, as you get closer to your date of travel, I recommend that you check any potential closing dates of the main landmarks that you'll visit. That's because some of them, such as the Notre-Dame Cathedral, might be closed for planned renovations. Other landmarks might also be closed during public holidays. Knowing all that info ahead of time will help you modify your trip and avoid any potential disappointment.

Also, if you haven't done so already, make sure you download the complimentary PDF guide so you have a nice visual of the different paths you will take.

Visit the following page to download your free bonus:

www.thecouchmanager.com/piwbonus

Finally, remember that FOMO (Fear of Missing Out) and FOBO (Fear of Better Options) are your enemies during your journey. The best trips are about who you're *with* and not about what you *do*. Even if things don't go 100% according to plan, don't lose focus on the big picture: you're in Paris and this is a vacation.

So enjoy it with your family.

Two Quick Requests!

I'd like to thank you once again for purchasing this book. I hope you found it helpful, and I wish you the best on your trip.

A couple of quick requests:

1) Please review the book on Amazon

If you enjoyed the book, please leave an honest review about it on Amazon. I know you probably get asked this a lot from most authors. However, every single review counts, and it would help me understand how to improve in my future books. Writing a review takes as little as sixty seconds, and, if you're unsure of what to write, let me know how one thing in this book has helped you. I read every single review and sincerely appreciate your feedback.

2) Check out my other book: "Rome in a Weekend with Two Kids"

If you enjoyed reading this book, then you'll love my other book, *Rome in a Weekend with Two Kids.* It's written in the exact same style as this book and gives you a great step-by-step itinerary of what you can do around the city. I also highlight the absolute best places for gelato, as well as where to go to learn how to make your own Italian pizza with your kids.

You can find the book on Amazon by searching for *Rome in a Weekend with Two Kids* in the search bar.

Thanks again!

Hassan

Would you like to write a book like this one?

This is my second travel book, and I wrote it while being a full-time employee, a full-time father, and a full-time procrastinator.

Writing a book is a process that's a lot easier than most people think.

In fact, I've written three other books as a part-time author.

If you would like to write a book like this one yourself, check out my latest Amazon #1 Best Seller:

Write Your Book on the Side: How to Write and Publish Your First Nonfiction Kindle Book While Working a Full-Time Job *(Even if You Don't Have a Lot of Time and Don't Know Where to Start)*

Here's what a few people have said about it:

"As a full-time Harvard Trauma surgeon, a full-time researcher and a full-time father of 3, I do not have the time to write a book on the side. Or so I thought. This book completely challenged my misconceptions

and deeply motivated me to write a book myself."
- Dr. Haytham Kaafarani, Assistant Professor of Surgery, Harvard Medical School

"Publishing your own book will help you clarify the message you want the world to hear. This concise, smart read shows you exactly how to do it, step-by-step."
- Dave Stachowiak, Host of the "Coaching for Leaders" podcast

"Highly readable, accessible, and positive, with practical tips and a systematic framework for the writing and publishing process."
- Rob Archangel, Owner and Co-founder of "Archangel Ink"

Visit the following link to check out my "Write Your Book on the Side" book:

www.thecouchmanager.com/bookontheside

Printed in Great Britain
by Amazon